P9-CFS-512

AWESOME JOKES

THAT EVERY
9 YEAR OLD
SHOULD KNOW

Copyright © 2018 by Say So Media Ltd.

All rights reserved.

No part of this book may be reproduced in any form or by any electronic or mechanical means including information storage and retrieval systems, without permission in writing from the author.

Names, characters, places, and products are used fictitiously. Any resemblance to actual persons, living or dead, events, or locales is entirely coincidental. If you can't make your parents laugh with these jokes, maybe you need new parents?

Depending on where you live, some spellings might seem odd to you like colour, or favourite. I've done it on purpose: I'm aktually quite good at spelling. OK, it's because I'm from England and I'm no good at baseball jokes. Just skip over the ones you don't understand, and I hope you enjoy the others!

Joke research: Olivera Ristovska

Design: Fanni Williams / thehappycolourstudio.com
Icons made by: Freepik from www.flaticon.com

www.matwaugh.co.uk

Produced by Big Red Button Books,
a division of Say So Media Ltd.

ISBN: 978-1-9999147-5-2

Published: May 2018
This edition: July 2019

AWESOME JOKES

9 THAT EVERY YEAR OLD SHOULD KNOW

MAT WAUGH
ILLUSTRATIONS BY EVGENIYA AVERINA

Introduction

What makes you laugh?

I saw a video of a dog on a skateboard. That made me chuckle.

My big sister once put invisible wrap over the toilet. My dad didn't see it and the pee bounced all over the bathroom. We *all* laughed at that – except Dad. And then my sister, when he made her clean it up. Disgusting.

This book is full of all the best jokes I know. Use them to find out which grown-ups are fun, and which ones are probably dead.

Or just tell them to your friends. I did!

PS Know a better one? Get it on the World Map of Awesome Jokes! See the back pages.

Let's Get Cracking!

What did one rock pool say to another?
Show us your mussels!

**My friend got crushed by a pile of books.
He's only got his shelf to blame.**

 **Who's the toughest card player in the band?**
The drummer, because she'll beat anyone!

Which hand should you use to pick up a rattlesnake?
Someone else's!

 **I feel like a racehorse.**
Take one of these every four laps. You'll soon be in a stable condition.

 **Knock Knock!**

Who's there?
Handsome.
Handsome who?
Handsome fries to me please,
I'm starving!

What did one magnet say to the other?

I find you highly attractive!

DOCTOR, DOCTOR! ✚

I keep thinking I'm a burglar!
Have you taken anything for it?

What do you call a snappy detective who wears a sleeveless t-shirt?
An in-vest-i-gator!

What is black and white, black and white, black and white?
A penguin falling down the stairs!

How do you make an octopus laugh?
Use ten-tickles!

What word begins with an E, ends with an E but only has one letter in it?
An envelope.

 **Could you help me out?**
Certainly, which way did you come in?

Why did Dracula take his medicine?

To help his coffin!

I've got amnesia.
Just go home and try to forget about it.
Forget about what?

DOCTOR, DOCTOR! **I keep thinking I'm a caterpillar.**
Don't worry, change is on the way!

What do you call a robot that always takes the long route round?
R2 detour!

Waiter, Waiter! **There is a fly in my salad!**
I'm sorry sir, you should have told me you're a vegetarian!

DOCTOR, DOCTOR! **Everyone thinks I'm a liar.**
I've never heard such rubbish!

What do elves use to make sandwiches?

Shortbread!

What is the difference between a jeweller and a jailer?

A jeweller sells watches and a jailer watches cells!

What's a strict teacher's favourite puzzle?

A crossword!

What do elves learn at school?

The elf-a-bet!

Knock Knock!

Who's there?
Europe.
Europe who?
No you're a poo!

My editor: You're not really putting that poo joke in, are you?
Sure, I said.
It's the best joke in the book!

What did the hat say to the scarf?

You go on ahead, I'll hang around.

Why did the two number 4s skip lunch?
They already 8.

Knock Knock!

Who's there?
Disguise!
Disguise who?
Disguise the limit!

DOCTOR, DOCTOR! ➕ **I keep thinking I'm a woodworm.**
How boring for you!

TONGUE TWISTER

Try and get your lips round this one!
My sister's shop sells shoes for sheep.

Why couldn't the teddy bear eat his ice cream?
He was completely stuffed!

Who's there?
Alex!
Alex who?
Alex the questions round here!

 **I think I'm suffering from déjà vu!**
Didn't I see you yesterday?

What's the difference between a pizza and this joke?

There's no topping this joke!

Knock Knock!

Who's there?
Interrupting cow.
Interrupting co....

MOO!

What kind of driver has no arms or legs?
A screwdriver!

Knock Knock!

Who's there?
X.
X who?
X-tremely pleased to meet you!

Where do knights learn to kill dragons?

At knight school!

What do astronauts wear to keep warm?
Apollo-neck sweaters!

What did the chef say when she forgot to put beef on the menu?
I think I've made a big miss-steak...

 **DOCTOR, DOCTOR!** ➕ **I think I'm an electric eel.**
Goodness, that's shocking!

 **Who's there?**
Poppy!
Poppy who?
Poppy-n anytime you like!

 **Why are snakes hard to fool?**
You can't pull their leg!

TONGUE TWISTER

(This twister is disgusting!)
The fat farmer's five filthy fingers fed the ferocious ferret french fries.

How do you know when it's cold outside?
When you milk a brown cow you get chocolate ice cream!

Why did the student do multiplication problems on the floor?
The teacher told him not to use tables.

Knock Knock!

Who's there?
Chicken.
Chicken who?
Chicken your pockets, I can't find my keys!

DOCTOR, DOCTOR! ➕

Will I be able to play the violin after the operation?
Yes, of course...
Great! I never could before!

What's the first noise of the day?
The crack of dawn!

Knock Knock!

Who's there?
Nun.
Nun who?
Nun of your business!

**What are the two strongest
days of the week?**
Saturday and Sundays. Because the
other days are week days.

**What do you call a cow on
a trampoline?**
A milk shake!

Knock Knock!

Who's there?
Accordion.
Accordion who?
Accordion to the radio,
it's going to rain tonight.

Why can't you trust atoms?
They make up everything!

**Why did the child study
in the airplane?**
He wanted a higher education!

Why did the
koala get
fired?

He only did
the bear
minimum!

**DOCTOR,
DOCTOR!**

I keep seeing double!
How interesting. Please take
a chair.
Which one?

**What is a cheerleader's
favourite colour?**
Yeller!

Who's there?
Olive.
Olive who?
Aah, how sweet!
I love you too!

You'll think this one is easy. But it's not. Or if it is, you should have your own YouTube channel.
Sheena leads, Sheila needs.

TONGUE TWISTER

How do books like to sleep?
Under the covers!

What do you call a snake without any clothes?

Snaked!

Why do spiders know everything?
Because they're always on the web!

What's the fastest way to become a stuntman?
Apply for a crash course!

Chester.
Chester who?
**Chester minute,
don't you recognise me?**

Why did the man put his money in the freezer?
He wanted some cold hard cash.

Jolly juggling jesters jauntily juggled jingling jacks.

TONGUE TWISTER

DOCTOR, DOCTOR!

I feel like a pony.
Don't worry, you're just a little hoarse!

Where do sharks go on holiday?

Finland!

What do you call a thief who steals pigs?
A ham-burglar!

Why did the silly scientist remove his doorbell?
He wanted to win the no-bell peace prize.

Who's there?
Bless!
Bless who?
I didn't sneeze!

Did you hear about the kidnapping?

She woke up.

Who's there?
Doctor.
Doctor who?
Correct, now open up! I can't find my sonic screwdriver!

Never watched Doctor Who? Google it!

 **How did the mouse say goodbye?**
With a micro-wave!

What do donkeys do in the morning?

Hold an assembly!

Who solved crimes but couldn't drink soup?
Sherlock Bones!

 **Why do pictures of hippos take up so much space on your Dad's phone?**
Because every one is a mega-byte!

Why did the picture go to jail?
Because it had been framed!

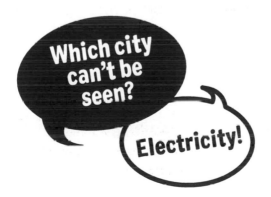

I'm so bright my mother calls me son.

The teacher pointed his ruler at the student. "At the end of this ruler there is an idiot!" he thundered.
"Which end?" asked the student.

 **Why don't spies break wind in bed?** Because they don't want to blow their cover.

Who's there?
Guinea!
Guinea who?
Guinea a break!

First astronaut: I'm hungry.
Second astronaut: So am I, it must be launch time!

What drink can you make in your pocket on a sunny day?

Hot chocolate!

In a lesson about babies, the teacher asked her class a question. "What were you before you came to school, boys and girls?" **"Happy!" they all cried out.**

Waiter, Waiter!

Is there soup on the menu?
No, madam, I wiped
most of it off.

**Who's in charge of a cemetery
on public holidays?**
Just a skeleton crew.

**why isn't this joke punctuated
properly?**
my editor doesn't believe in capital
punishment.

**Knock
Knock!**

Who's there?
Safari!
Safari who?
Safari so good!

**Why were the early days of history
called the dark ages?**
Because there were so many knights.

"I told you to draw a picture of a cow eating grass," said the teacher. **"Where's the grass?"**
"The cow ate it."
"And where's the cow?"
"It left because there wasn't any grass."

Which soldiers smell of salt and pepper?
Seasoned ones!

I tried to buy some camouflage trousers the other day but I couldn't find any.

This joke is terrible. It really has no plaice in this book.

Who's there?
Halibut.
Halibut who?
Halibut you let me inside!

What instrument do skeletons play?
The trombone.

What do you call a ghost's mum and dad?

Transparents!

There is a fly in my soup!
What did you expect for this price, a bald eagle?

What's worse than a shower of frogs?
Hailing taxis!

What do you get when a dinosaur scores a touchdown?
A dino-score!

What travels at 100mph underground?
A mole in a sports car!

Who's there?
Radio!
Radio who?
Radio not, here I come!

Pupil: Would you punish me for something I didn't do?
Teacher: Of course not.
Pupil: Good, because I haven't done my homework.

What do you call a group of disorganized cats?
A cat-astrophe!

Knock Knock!

Who's there?
Padme.
Padme who?
Padme down if you have to, but let me in!

What does a spy do when he gets cold?
He goes undercover.

Why did the woman go outdoors with her purse open?
Because she expected some change in the weather!

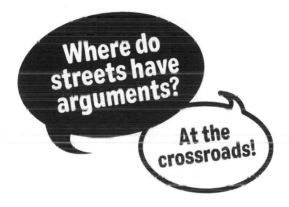

Where do streets have arguments?

At the crossroads!

What did the calculator say to the maths student?
You can count on me.

Why can't pirates remember the alphabet?
Because they always get lost at C!

Which wrist watches are Swiss wrist watches?

TONGUE TWISTER

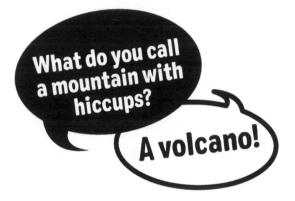

What do you call a mountain with hiccups?

A volcano!

A skeleton orders a drink and takes a sip. "Do you need anything else?" asks the barman. The skeleton looks down. "Maybe a mop?"

I tried to catch some fog earlier. I mist.

When do doctors get mad?
When they run out of patients.

 **Why did the burglar finish his homework early?**
He'd only been given a short sentence.

What is a ghost's favourite food?
Ghoulash!

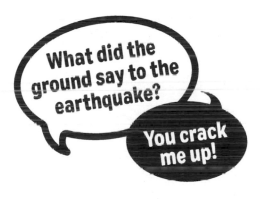

What did the ground say to the earthquake?

You crack me up!

What do you get when you mix the chemicals Ba and Na²?
A banana!
This is a science joke. If you get it you're 100% genius.

What kind of vegetable do plumbers fix?
Leeks!

What do authors like to nibble?
A battered copy of their favourite book!

**What starts with a T,
ends with a T, and is full of T?**
A teapot!

Why did the pillow go to the doctor?
He was feeling all stuffed up!

Why are astronauts successful people?
Because they're always going up
in the world !

My fear of moving stairs is escalating.

What do you call Chewbacca when he has chocolate stuck in his hair?
Chocolate Chip Wookee.

What do you get when you cross a teacher with a vampire?
Daily blood tests!

What do you call Santa Claus in a spaceship?
A U-F-HO-HO-HO!

 The police have arrested a bike for the third time. They say it's a vicious cycle.

How did Thor build his house?
With thunderbolts.

Why is a computer so smart?
Because it always listens to its
motherboard.

What was the first thing Count Dracula wanted to see when he went to New York?
The Vampire State Building.

A child threw a lump of cheddar at me. 'That's not very mature,' I thought.

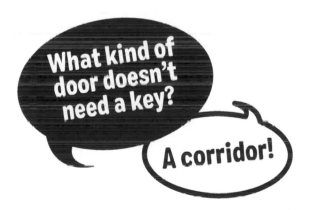

What kind of door doesn't need a key?

A corridor!

Why did the Loch Ness Monster fail all his exams?
Because he didn't believe in himself.

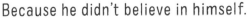

EVERYONE LOVES A GOOD NAME JOKE...

What do you call a woman with one leg?
Eileen!

What do you call a woman with no legs?
Nolene!

What do you call a man with no shins?

Neil!

What do you call a man with a spade on his head?
Doug!

What do you call a man *without* a spade on his head?
Douglas!

What do you call a man who's good at home improvements?
Andy!

What do you call a man who smells of gravy?
Stu!

What do you call a man who always wins?
Victor!

What do you call a man who holds back water?
Adam!

What do you call a man who gets you into trouble?
Adair!

What do you call a man in a pile of leaves?
Russell!

Want more? turn over!

What do you call a man
floating in the sea?
Bob!

What do you call a woman who looks like
a radiator ?
Anita!

What do you call a
woman with tiles on
her head?

Ruth!

What do you call a woman who often breaks
wind?
Gail!

What do you call a woman who loves tortoises?
Shelley!

What do you call a woman with a toilet?
Lou!

What do you call a woman with two toilets?
Lulu!

What do you call a man with excellent eyesight?
Seymour!

What do you call a man attacked by a tiger?
Claude!

What do you call a girl who always has her hand up?
Mimi!

Phew - that's enough for now!

What do you call a chef in a hurry?

A pressure cooker!

What did the polar bear say when it saw a seal on a bike?
Yummy, meals on wheels!

Why did Eve want to move to New York?
She fell for the Big Apple.

What is 5Q + 5Q?
10Q (And you're welcome!)

Waiter, Waiter!

What do you call this?
That's bean soup, sir.
I don't care what it's been, what is it now?

 Will and Bill were arguing about whose Dad was best.
"My father's the one who dug the hole for the Pacific Ocean," said Will.
"That's rubbish," said Bill. "My Dad's the one who killed the Dead Sea!"

What do funky vampires carry for protection?
A nightclub.

How do angry people tie their shoes?
With a crossbow.

Why did the book join the police?

He wanted to go undercover!

What do you call a small leaf?

A leaflet!

What does the president ask for when he goes to the barbershop?
A power cut.

What vegetable do librarians like?
Quiet peas!

Did you hear about the woman who mounted a lion's head on her bedroom wall?
The décor-ate-her.

Why does history keep repeating itself?
Because we weren't listening the first time!

The wisest joke in this book

Teacher: Where is the English Channel?
Student: I don't know, my TV doesn't pick it up!

How do you catch a school of fish?
With bookworms!

What do you call a skeleton who won't get up in the morning?
Lazy bones!

What did one plate say to the other?
The dinner's on me tonight.

What kind of trousers do ghosts wear?
Boo-jeans!

What does an octopus wear when it gets cold?
A coat of arms!

Who's there?
Thumb!
Thumb who?
Thumb one who'd like to get in out of the cold!

Why did the actor kill the oak tree?
Because every time he saw it he took a bough.

What's the saddest fruit in the world?
Blueberry.

Who do poets call in an emergency?

The serious rhyme squad!

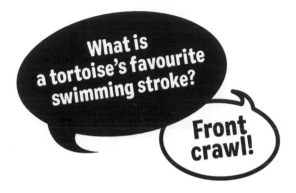

What is a tortoise's favourite swimming stroke?

Front crawl!

Is it a history lesson or a tongue twister? You decide!
A Tudor who tooted a flute tried to tutor two tooters to toot. Said the two to their tutor, "Is it harder to toot or to tutor two tooters to toot?"

TONGUE TWISTER

What did the tornado say to the sports car?
Want to go for a spin?

What goes tick-tock, woof-woof, tick-tock, woof-woof?
A watch dog.

 **Last year's omelette festival makes a terrible mess. Police have called for a crackdown.**

It's very stressful for the organizer. People say he's cracking up.

It's such a shame; it used to be egg-cellent.

With yolks like that I'm surprised you're still henjoying this book.

Who's there?
Broken pencil!
Broken pencil who?
Oh forget it, there's no point!

My food is trapped inside this glass box!
That's right, sir, this is the obstacle course.

Why do Eskimos win at poker?
Because they always play it cool.

I keep thinking I'm a bell.
Well just go home and if you don't feel better, give me a ring.

What is a cat's favourite movie?
The Sound of Mew-sic!

What is a witch's favourite class?
Spelling!

Who's there?
Zippy!
Zippy who?
Mrs Zippy!

Why do elephants paint their toenails?
To hide in a bag of M&Ms!

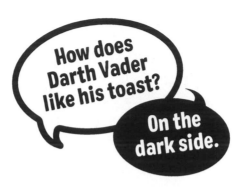

How does
Darth Vader
like his toast?

On the
dark side.

If leather makes shoes, what does a banana make?
Slippers!

Why did the burglar have a shower?
To make a clean getaway!

 **Police report that several Siamese kittens have gone missing. They say it's a copycat crime.**

Why did the circle turn round?
The triangle showed her acute angle.

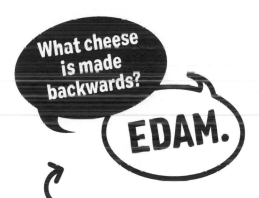

What cheese is made backwards?

EDAM.

You might have to think about this one! Need a clue? Read the answer from right to left...

 **I feel like a pack of cards.**
I'll deal with you later!

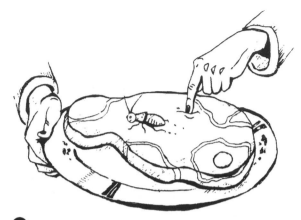

Waiter, Waiter!

You've got your finger on my steak!
I know, sir. I don't want it to fall on the floor again.

The great Greek grape growers grow great Greek grapes.

TONGUE TWISTER

DOCTOR, DOCTOR!

Every time I stand up quickly, I see Mickey Mouse, Donald Duck and Goofy.
I see. How long have you been getting these Disney spells?

 **Why couldn't the pirate play cards?**
Because he was sitting on the deck!

Did you hear about the earthquake over at the apple farm last week? People say the farmer was shaken to the core.

 **Who's there?**
Sacha!
Sacha who?
Sacha fuss, just because I knocked on your door.

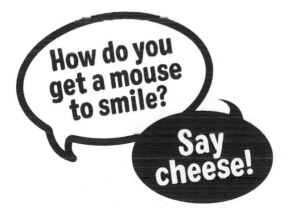

What animal is no fun at parties?

A wild boar!

Why did the sleepy driver crash into the wall?
Because he didn't break in time.

Knock Knock!

Who's there?
Sicily!
Sicily who?
Sicily question, let me in!

Where do they get the timber to make deckchairs?
From a beech tree!

Why didn't the skeleton turn up for work?
He had been arrested for a grave crime.

Knock Knock!

Who's there?
Sofa!
Sofa who?
Sofa so good!

Why did the artist sit naked in the town square?
He liked to draw a large crowd.

I ordered a stone ruler from a website last week. I asked about delivery and they've told me to expect a long weight.

What's the queen's favourite weather?

Reign!

If onions cry their eyes out, what do they become?
Onons!

Why did the racing car driver sell his house?
He'd run out of vroom.

Knock Knock!

Who's there?
Snow.
Snow who?
Snow business like show business!

What do you get when you cross a sheep and a kangaroo?
A woolly jumper!

Why shouldn't you ask a footballer to help you with a jigsaw?
Because they always take the corners!

How do you stop Grandma from smelling?
Put a peg on her nose!

WE'RE BACK WITH MORE NAME JOKES!

What do you call a girl on a beach?
Sandy!

What do you call a woman who's hard to see?
Heidi!

What do you call a man who's always exercising?

Jim!

What do you call a woman who can jump across huge gaps?
Bridget!

What do you call a woman with a sun bed shop?
Tanya!

What do you call a man with a bug on his head?
Anton!

What do you call a woman with a bottle of toilet unblocker?
Louise!

What do you call a man with rabbits down his pants?
Warren!

What do you call a woman who loves hanging out the washing?
Peggy!

What do you call a man with a car on his head?
Jack!

What do you call a man you wipe your dirty feet on?
Mat.
(Humph. I don't find this joke funny.)

What type of star goes to jail?
A shooting star!

Knock Knock!

Who's there?
Wah!
Wah who?
Steady now, you don't have to get so excited about it!

What weather terrifies scarecrows?

A cold snap!

Why is it hard to keep a crowd of snowmen entertained?
They always melt away.

What type of jokes do chiropodists like?

Corny ones!

Why did the athlete become a politician?
Because he wanted to run the country!

TONGUE TWISTER
Six sick hicks nick six slick bricks with picks and sticks.

What does a chef wear when it gets chilly?

A cooker hood!

What is the highest digit?
An astro-naught!

Fitting a moving staircase in your house is a mistake because the cost is always escalating.

Get a quote for a lift instead. It'll go up, but you should be able to get it down again.

Or you could ask about the price of a hot air balloon, but watch out: it's bound to rise.

What do you call a close relative who keeps getting expelled from school?
Your first cousin twice removed.

What do you get if you cross a cat with a dark horse?
Kitty Perry!

Who's there?
Alice!
Alice who?
Alice fair in love and war!

What's the hairiest thing in the forest?

A fir tree!

Knock Knock!

Who's there?
Oswald!
Oswald who?
Oswald my false teeth...

What's the saddest time of the day?

Mourning.

A man in a boiler suit came to my house earlier. "I should warn you, I charge a lot for a leek," he said. "Why is that?" I asked. "I bought a sack of carrots for almost nothing last week."
"Yes, but I'm a plumber."

Why has Tony the Tiger asked for police protection?
There's a cereal killer on the loose.

Waiter, Waiter!

This coffee is terrible – it tastes like mud!
Yes sir, it was ground yesterday.

Which sport takes the longest time to play?
Snooker, because there's always a queue.

How do you get a cake to fly?
Make it with plane flour.

Did you hear about the shoplifting chicken?
He was locked up for fowl deeds.

Why did the man give all his friends a set of rubber stamps just before he died?
Because he wanted to leave a lasting impression.

What's a farmer's favourite treat?
Cotton candy!
*(Scratching your head over this one?
You might call it candy floss!)*

Tommy the acrobat hung upside down for 3 days using just his toes. People couldn't believe his amazing feat.

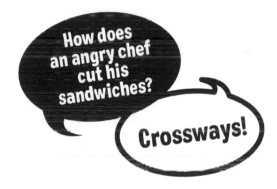

How does an angry chef cut his sandwiches?

Crossways!

Why don't people build houses below dams?
Because nobody wants to live under a curse.

At the back of my local dried fruit shop there's a sign:
Beware: Dangerous Currants.

Which hand does an author always use?

His write hand!

What's the most religious creature on earth?
A bird of pray!

DOCTOR, DOCTOR! **I've lost my memory!**
When did this happen?
When did what happen?
Who are you?

There's a sale on at the pet shop. All the budgies are going cheep.

What's the nickname for a king's wig?
The heir to the crown.

**What do you get if you cross a pig
with a dinosaur ?**
Jurassic Pork!

**What do apple farmers do in the
middle of the day?**
Stop for crunch.

 **Which section of the
orchestra knows the
most emojis?**
Percussion, because they're
great with cymbals.

What's better than gym class?

Skipping lessons!

Why did the wolf cough?
He had a hare stuck in his throat.

Did you hear about the snooker player who tripped?
He fell right on cue.

Waiter, Waiter!

There's no chicken in this chicken pie!
That's right sir, and there's no dog in a hot dog, so why are you complaining?

When should you call in the dinner detectives?
When you want to find the sauce of a leek.

Why did Jake find a jumbo jet outside his bedroom door?
His Dad had left the landing light on!

Who's there?
Eyesore.
Eyesore who?
Eyesore do like you!

What's the quickest way to cover up a bald spot?

Cut and paste!

Did you hear about the parents who threw pudding at each other? They were locked in a custardy battle.

 **I think I'm starting to look like a toilet.**
Ah yes! Now you mention it you do seem a bit flushed.

What does an owl do when you tell it a joke?
Hoots with laughter!

Which dog always wins the race?
The one with the comfortable lead.

I've been waiting in this hot room for ages! I'm boiling up!
Just simmer down, I'll see you soon!

Why are books about frogs scary?
Because the pictures really leap off the page.

She sold six shabby sheared sheep on a ship.

A snake can slither up stairs but it can't stand escalators.

What happens when you wrong person?

You're making a grave mistake!

Why was the chimney sweep fired?
He kept giving his customers dirty looks.

Did you hear about the sandpaper salesman?
He got a bonus for his abrasive manner!

Weathermen are well known for their stormy meetings.

DOCTOR, DOCTOR!

I can't tell the truth!
I suggest you go and lie on that couch over there.

Why do firemen carry rulers?
In case they need to take emergency measures.

What's a frog's favourite saying?
Time's fun when you're having flies!

Why do chicken farmers make the best spies?
Because they always scramble their messages.

Who's there?
Heidi!
Heidi who?
Heidi-clare war on you!

Which circus performers can see in the dark?
The acro-bats!

I like all my pets,
but the one I love most is my deer.

 **I think I'm shrinking.**
Well take these tablets, but you'll have to be a little patient.

Why do fishermen make the best actors?
Because they never forget their lines.

 **Why is it hard to catch a window cleaner's eye?**
Because of his glazed look.

Did you hear about the award-winning window cleaner?
He went straight to the top of the glass!

Famous Chinese proverb: Salt fine, but cheese grater

 **Who's there?**
Ringo!
Ringo who?
Ringo-f truth!

 **Knock Knock!**

Who's there?
Wooden.
Wooden who?
Wooden you like to know!

Why did the man forget to buy soap?

It slipped his mind!

What do giants wear around their necks?
A chain of mountains!

What do you call a cow with no feet?
Ground beef.

Knock Knock!

Who's there?
Annie.
Annie who?
Annie thing you can do,
I can do better!

**What happened to the clown who ran
away with the circus?**
The police made him bring it back.

What's the greediest creature in the forest?

A goblin!

Where should you look for giant snails?
At the end of giant's fingers.

Why did the chef throw his laptop out of the window?
He could never find the right menu.

Nothing succeeds like a parrot with no teeth.

How will an athlete give directions?
He'll draw you a quick map.

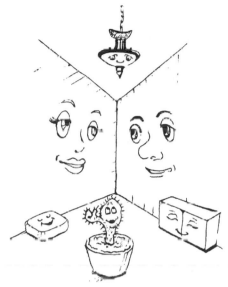

What did one wall say to the other wall?
I'll meet you at the corner.

How do you build a house out of sunshine?

Use sunbeams!

How does a builder request extra bricks?

Mor-tar!

What's the smallest drum in the world?
Your eardrum.

What did the computer do at snack time?
It had a quick byte!

 **Who's there?**
Cows go.
Cows go who?
No, cows go moo!

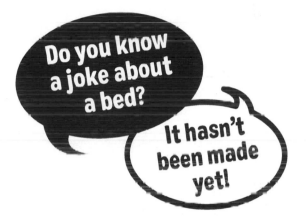

Do you know a joke about a bed?

It hasn't been made yet!

 **DOCTOR, DOCTOR!** **My wife thinks she's a lift!**
Tell her to come in, let's take a look at her.
I can't. She doesn't stop at this floor!

What's big, purple and smells horrible?
A monster's bottom.

 **I think I'm a phone!**
How strange. Take these tablets and if they don't work then give me a ring!

What's the capital of Germany?

G!

Why did the diner order a cardboard box?
Because he wanted a square meal!

Why did the diner order a helium balloon?
Because he wanted a light bite!

Why did the diner ask for some scales?
Because he wanted a balanced menu!

What do you call two petty thieves?
A pair of knickers.

**Why didn't Snow White hear the
dwarves come home?**
Because they made a low-key entrance.

What do pigs say before they take-off?
Chops away!

Why did the chicken cross the road?
To get to the other – *hang on, this joke shouldn't be here. It should be in the book for five year olds! Let's see if we can do any better...*

Why did the chicken cross the playground?
To get to the other slide!

What do you call a joke book for chickens?

A yolk book!

Which side of a chicken has the most feathers?
The outside.

What do you get if you cross a doll with a hen?
Barbie-Q-chicken!

How does a chicken blow his nose?
With a henkerchief!

Why did the chicken cross the road again?
He was trying to fetch his boomerang!

Why did the chewing gum cross the road?
It was stuck to the chicken's foot!

Why did the goat cross the road?
It was the chicken's day off!

What do you get if you cross a chicken with a cement mixer?
A brick-layer!

That's quite enough chicken jokes!

Where do otters keep their money?

In a riverbank!

Did you hear about the man who trod in a sieve?
He strained his ankle.

What's the biggest show-off in the ocean?
A starfish.

Who never misses an ocean party?
A jellyfish.

DOCTOR, DOCTOR!

I think I'm a yo-yo.
Don't worry, you'll bounce back
in the morning!

 **I think horses make great neighbours.**
Not mine: they're nightmares!

What time do ghosts get up?
In the dead of night!

Where do Eskimos keep their money?
In a snow bank!

 Hang on, that's cheating: it's just like the otter joke on the opposite page!

**How did they announce the
pancake competition on TV?**
Breaking news!

How did they announce the forest fire?
Hot news.

**How did they announce the delayed Justin
Timberlake concert?**
Late news, just in.

**How did they announce the photography
convention?**
With a news flash.

**How did they report the return of the
gorilla to the wild?**
With a news release.

How did they find out about the plumber's strike?
There was a news leak.

 **How do you make friends with a burglar?**
Use his nickname.

What do you get If you cross a sweet potato and a jazz musician?
A yam session!
If you understand this joke you are probably a farmer that likes jazz music. And that's quite impressive for a nine year old.

How does a cutlery factory stack their boxes?
With a forklift truck!

Now it's your turn!

The most awesome jokes sent in by 9-year-olds from around the world. (Can you do better? See page 101!)

Why did the eye go to school?
Because it was a pupil!
(From Sophie, Sawston)

Sent in by Ella, aged 9, from Shenfield

Why did the baker have brown hands?
Because he kneaded a poo!

There were two cats about to race across the channel. One called One Two Three and the other called Un Deux Trois. Which one do you think won?
(From Eve, Kent)
Warning: this is a joke for very intelligent people who speak French, like Eve. I didn't get it.

What are the strongest days of the week?
Saturday and Sunday, because the others are week days!
(From Kian, Tunbridge Wells)

How do you stop a cute dog video?
Press the paws button!
(From James, Edinburgh)

What do you call a dear with no ear?
D!
(From Charlotte, Reading)

How does a skeleton call his friends?
On the tele-bone!
(From Mataya, England)

Mix and match!

Can you match each joke to its punchline? But watch out: there are two questions missing! You'll find them in **More Awesome Jokes Every 9 Year Old Should Know** – buy it now!

Where's the best place to get a massage?

How do weight-lifters give directions?

How do butchers end their day?

What does an emperor do after breakfast?

Why did the golfer get sunburn?

What do you call a launchpad for kittens?

Who's never late to the theatre?

Hmm! What can it mean?

K	X	S	B	R	I	L	L	I	A	N	T
K	I	S	Q	W	J	I	X	N	P	I	O
Y	O	T	E	R	C	E	S	C	Q	M	I
W	N	P	L	C	E	A	S	E	R	E	E
R	A	T	E	T	A	H	I	E	C	S	H
S	B	O	O	K	O	N	V	N	H	S	T
A	M	A	Z	O	N	O	T	O	I	A	M
A	K	E	M	E	C	H	A	P	L	G	P
Y	Q	Q	O	S	T	U	T	O	D	E	A
K	V	N	I	E	J	O	G	G	R	E	P
M	L	D	V	M	C	Q	B	L	E	E	L
Y	B	C	P	O	P	D	R	Z	N	W	F

1. BRILLIANT   4. DISCOVER   7. SECRET
2. CAN   5. MESSAGE   8. THE
3. CHILDREN   6. ONLY

I know a great joke!

Send me your best joke and I'll put it on my **World Map of Awesome Jokes**!

Head over to the map now to discover silly jokes, clever jokes and weird jokes. Some jokes rhyme, some are a crime, but they're all sent in by children like you!

Will you be the first on the map from your town?

Put your awesome joke here at
www.matwaugh.co.uk/jokemap

About Mat Waugh

It's funny what makes you laugh, isn't it? Sometimes it's a great joke, and I hope you found a few in this book. Sometimes you don't even need words. It could be a funny look from a friend in class. Or maybe it's something that wasn't supposed to happen.

Once, when I was about your age, I was in the back of my aunt's car on a Christmas Day. The sun reflected brightly in the deep puddles from the night's rain.

My aunt wasn't very good at driving. As we approached a dip in the road we could see a vicar cycling towards us, on his way to church. Dad told my aunt to slow down... but she pressed the wrong pedal. The car hit the water with a mighty SPLOOSH! I looked back to see a huge wave swamping the vicar and his bike. He shook his fists at us, but my aunt didn't even notice. I'm still laughing... but I bet the vicar isn't.

I have three daughters to make me laugh now. (Not all the time though: they drive me bananas.)

I live in Tunbridge Wells, which is a lively, lovely town in the south east of England. It's not a very funny place, mind you..

I've always written a lot. I've done lots of writing for other people – mostly serious stuff – but now I write silly, crazy and funny books as well.

Talking of crazy, I had a mad year when I thought I wanted to be a teacher. But then I found out how hard teachers work and that you have to buy your own biscuits. So now I just visit schools to eat their snacks and talk to children about stories.

Last thing: I love hearing from readers. Thoughts, jokes... anything. If that's you, then get in touch.

✉ mail@matwaugh.co.uk
www.matwaugh.co.uk

Or, if you're old enough:

 facebook.com/matwaughauthor
twitter.com/matwaugh

Three more to try!

Cheeky Charlie vol 1-6

Meet Harriet and her small, stinky brother. Together, they're trouble. Fabulously funny stories for kids aged 6 and up.

Fantastic Wordsearches

Wordsearch with a difference: themed, crossword clues and hidden words await!

The Fun Factor

When the fun starts vanishing, it seems Thora is the only one to notice. The headmaster is definitely up to no good, but what about Dad's new girlfriend? A mystery adventure for gadget-loving kids aged 8 and up.

Available from Amazon and local bookshops.

MORE
AWESOME JOKES
FOR 9 YEAR OLDS
OUT NOW!

Be the first to know about new stuff! Sign up for my emails at matwaugh.co.uk

Made in the USA
Middletown, DE
21 August 2020

16269501R00064